Simple SUPERNATURAL

KEYS TO LIVING IN THE GLORY REALM

Study Guide

JOSHUA S. MILLS

ISBN: 978-0-9830789-0-6

Published by
New Wine International, Inc.
www.NewWineInternational.org

Printed in the United States of America

TABLE OF CONTENTS

Introduction 5

You are Supernatural! 7

Signs & Wonders 15

Soul Winning in the Glory 29

Receive the Power! 37

Power to Heal the Sick 49

Seven Keys to the Glory Realm 61

The Commission 77

Study Guide Answers 83

INTRODUCTION

Before leaving the earth Jesus said, "Go into all the world" (Mark 16:15-20). Jesus didn't say to stay put, fasten your seatbelt, or to be comfortable in the church pew. He said to "Go!" This is the commission that He is giving you today. Jesus even said that you would do greater miracles than He did on the earth!

The purpose of this study guide is to facilitate greater understanding and personal application of the material in my book *Simple Supernatural* so you can "Go!" Each lesson in this study guide directly correlates to its respective chapter in the book. Additionally, most headers in this study guide align with the headers in the book. Answers to the study questions can be found in the back of the study guide.

I pray that as you go through this guide you feel the anointing of God filling you with His strength for supernatural soul winning, the baptism in the Holy Spirit, and the ability to go forth and heal the sick.

This is simple supernatural! Go and do it!!!

> *But don't just listen to God's word. You must do what it says. Otherwise, you are only fooling yourselves. – James 1:22 (NLT)*

Lesson One

YOU ARE SUPERNATURAL!

Objective: To understand that moving in supernatural power is simply living out your identity as a child of God.

Overview: Within this lesson you will search the Scriptures to learn what the Word of God says about moving in supernatural power.

 ## HIDDEN REVELATION

When I was in my late teenage years, my pastor often made us hold our Bibles and say, "I choose to believe my Bible on purpose!" What a powerful statement.

1. We have to believe our Bibles _____ _____!

The same level of miraculous provision and supernatural encounter is available for us today – at even greater levels!

2. Hebrews 13:8 says that Jesus Christ is the _____ – yesterday, today, and _____.

3. If we _____ what the Bible says, we will _____ what it tells us to do.

4. If we _____ what the Bible tells us to do, then we will get the _____ it says we can have.

NOTES

Because we believed God's Word:

5. We have laid hands on the sick and seen them miraculously _____.

    "They will place their hands on sick people, and they will get well." – Mark 16:18

6. We have cast out devils and set the demonic _____.

    "You, dear children, are from God and have overcome them, because the one who is in you is greater than the one who is in the world." – 1 John 4:4

7. We have spoken in other _____ and unknown _____.

    "I am the LORD your God, who brought you up out of Egypt. Open wide your mouth and I will fill it." – Psalm 81:10

Remarkable, creative miracles and supernatural phenomenon are being seen because the Word of God says that signs will follow those who believe (Mark 16:17), and we believe!

If you prosper in the Word, it will begin to prosper inside of you!

WHAT GOD SAYS ABOUT YOU

Look at the following Scriptures and see what God has said about you through His Word:

8. I have God's _____ of revelation in my _____!

    For God, who said, "Let light shine out of darkness," made his light shine in our hearts to give us the light of the knowledge of the glory of God in the face of Christ. – 2 Corinthians 4:6

9. I am _____ from all wickedness, _____ for God's possession, and _____ to do what is good!

    We wait for the blessed hope—the glorious appearing of our great God and Savior, Jesus Christ, who gave himself for us to redeem us from all wickedness and to purify for himself a people that are his very own, eager to do what is good. – Titus 2:13-14

NOTES

10. I have power and authority from God to drive out _____, speak in other _____, pick up _____ and drink _____ without harm, and _____ the sick!

> *"And these signs will accompany those who believe: In my name they will drive out demons; they will speak in new tongues; they will pick up snakes with their hands; and when they drink deadly poison, it will not hurt them at all; they will place their hands on sick people, and they will get well." After the Lord Jesus had spoken to them he was taken up into heaven and he sat at the right hand of God. Then the disciples went out and preached everywhere, and the Lord worked with them and confirmed his word by the signs that accompanied it. – Mark 16:17-20*

The Bible says that you are supernatural!

11. YOU are a supernatural _____, with a supernatural _____, which is to walk in the supernatural _____ _____ _____, while demonstrating God's supernatural Kingdom realities here on the earth!

> *But you are a chosen people, a royal priesthood, a holy nation, a people belonging to God, that you may declare the praises of him who called you out of darkness into his wonderful light. – 1 Peter 2:9*

The Bible says that we are citizens of another realm. Our true citizenship does not belong to a country of the earth, but we are actually citizens of another country. We are citizens of the Kingdom of God. We are aliens to the earth.

> *But our citizenship is in heaven. – Philippians 3:20*

12. Being *aliens* does not mean _____.

13. Being *aliens* means _____.

The Bible says that we are to be in the world but not a part of its ways. We are supposed to live from another dimension and that dimension is the glory realm.

14. In the glory realm we will produce greater _____!

Notes

KEYS FOR ACTIVATION

ARE YOU READY?

Ask yourself the following questions:

- **Are you ready to win souls in the glory?** The harvest is ready and it's waiting for you!

- **Are you ready to receive and minister the baptism in the Holy Spirit?** This supernatural power explosion is ready for you if you'll receive it and give it away!

- **Are you ready to heal the sick?** So many hurting people are waiting for somebody who will give them hope and bring answers to their problems!

If you answered yes to any or all of these questions:

- Let go of any preconceived ideas

- Ask and allow the Holy Spirit to lead you into the greatest days

- Pray out loud with me:

   Father God, right now I release to You all the preconceived ideas I have about the supernatural and how You want me to minister to others. Holy Spirit, I want to receive Your power and release it to those around me – those who are sick, hurting, and need real answers to their problems. Thank you for all that You've done in my life, and I know that my best days are still ahead because of Your supernatural work in my life. Amen!

 APPLICATION AT HOME

Statement of Declaration

Post the following statements somewhere in your home where you can read them each day this week (multiple times if possible). As you read and declare these powerful statements over the next week, the Word of God will come alive for you in a new way.

Declare these words out loud and begin to believe them in your heart.

- I choose to believe my Bible on purpose!

- I believe that I am who it says that I am!

- I believe that I have what it says I can have!

- And I can do what it says that I can do!

- I will let this Word become alive inside of me...

- ...so that I will become alive within the Word!

Lesson Two

SIGNS & WONDERS

Objective: To develop a paradigm for experiencing manifestations of God's glory and using them in ministry.

Overview: Within this lesson, you will hear testimonies of manifestations of God's glory and how they have opened doors for ministry.

 HIDDEN REVELATION

We've been experiencing the golden raindrops of God's glory for over a decade now, and I know that there is still so much more for the worldwide body of Christ!

1. The glory of God will ignite our ability to _____ the _____ and allow a great _____ of _____ to come forth.

2. In the past we have relied upon our own natural _____ and _____ to bring forth results.

3. We must learn how to flow in the _____ realm.

Just as the Lord sent manna to the children of Israel as their daily provision, so is the Lord releasing this unexplainable sign that represents heaven's prosperity and abundance.

Reflection:

• Describe how it would make you feel if you had gold dust manifest on you. If you have experienced this already, describe the experience you had.

NOTES

Just as Moses' face began to shine when he encountered God's presence on the mountain, and the Israelites saw God's glory before them as a vibrant flame and a dense cloud, the visible glory of God is appearing to His people in this day and hour.

Even though gold dust has become quite commonplace in our meetings, this unusual sign still makes us wonder! It causes us to think about the greatness of God. It turns our attention towards the glory and directs our eyes to Jesus Christ. If the Holy Spirit is able to take nothing and make something – taking the unseen and making it seen upon our hands, clothing, and Bibles – how much more will He do what He has promised to us within His Word!

Reflection:

- Write down the ways the sign and wonder of gold dust causes you to focus on or glorify God.

GOLD REPRESENTS THE GLORY OF GOD

Within the context of Scripture, gold represents the glory of God. We see this example in the symbolism of the Ark of the Covenant. The Ark was covered with the purest gold and represented the strength and glory of God. We also see this symbolism in the building of Solomon's temple - the walls and floors were overlaid with gold and also included golden ornamentation.

The New Testament tells us that God's temple is no longer one that has been built by the hands of man, but that God has chosen to display His glory through His people.

4. 1 Corinthians 3:16 says that you are God's _____ and His Spirit lives _____ you.

Reflection:

- If these signs and wonders are manifestations of God's glory that point us to Him, what specific purposes might they serve?

NOTES

GOD GIVES US GOLDEN OPPORTUNITIES

God gives us supernatural tools so that we will begin reaping a supernatural harvest of souls in the glory! He is releasing signs and wonders for the harvest!

5. Isaiah 55:8-9 says that God's _____ and _____ are higher than our own.

Reflection:

- Considering my "golden opportunity" in the elevator, do you believe that God will give you these kinds of opportunities?

- Have you noticed God setting more appointments for you the more you practice hearing His voice? Why do you think that is?

By the time we reached the lobby level, all three people had received Jesus Christ into their hearts. They explained to me that other people had shared the gospel with them before, but they had never seen a miracle like this in front of their eyes. They knew God was trying to get their attention.

Reflection:

- Think about your own salvation experience. How might your life as a Christian be different if it had started with signs and wonders?

NOTES

Signs will confirm the Word of God.

6. Mark 16:20 says that "the Lord worked _____ them and confirmed his word

    by the _____ that accompanied it.

We must allow the power of God's glory to work through us as we go into the harvest in the days ahead. We cannot bring in the multitudes with our efforts alone; we *must* be equipped with the power of God to bring forth the lost!

Reflection:

*   What does it mean to you that God will confirm His Word with signs, wonders, and miracles? What do you think that will look like in your life?

WORSHIP RELEASES THE GLORY OF GOD

7. As we worship, God's golden _____ rains down with droplets of salvation power!

GOD GIVES US GOLDEN TOOLS FOR A GOLDEN HARVEST

8. God's glory is always ever _____!

    But we all, with open face beholding as in a [mirror] the glory of the Lord, are changed into the same image from glory to glory, even as by the Spirit of the Lord. – 2 Corinthians 3:18 (KJV)

9. These visible manifestations of God's glory are "_____ signs" that carry a greater message than the sign themselves.

Notes

Reflection:

- What "love signs" have you seen as you have ministered to people?

- What fruit did they produce in those to whom you were ministering?

SIGNS AND WONDERS INCREASE OUR FAITH

After the resurrection, Jesus Christ appeared to His disciples. One of the first things that He did was to show them His nail-pierced hands and feet (Luke 24:40). Why did He do this? The Bible makes it clear that Jesus wanted the disciples to see the marks because they were a sign of His eternal love for them. Today the Lord is continuing to display wondrous signs as the Holy Spirit is being poured out all over the earth.

> *"In the last days," God says, "I will pour out my Spirit on all people…I will show wonders in the heaven above and signs on the earth below." – Acts 2:17, 19*

10. These signs cause us to pay attention to what God is _____, increase our _____, and are tokens of God's _____.

God's signs and wonders in the earth cause us to focus on the finished work of Jesus Christ and all that He has made available for us in the glory realm. These holy signs cause us to place our eyes on Jesus Christ as He is the Wonder of wonders!

Reflection:

- Signs *confirm* the Word of God, but what should you do if signs come *before* you receive or speak a word?

NOTES

Supernatural Oil

I believe that God wants to anoint us all with His miracle power to such a degree that we will be oozing with the love of God and His wonders everywhere we go!

11. 2 Corinthians 2:14-15 says that God always leads us in triumphal procession in Christ and through us spreads everywhere the _____ of the knowledge of Him.

12. This Scripture also says that we are the _____ of Christ to those who are being saved and those who are perishing.

13. Psalm 23:5 says that God _____ us with fresh _____, and our cups _____.

God did extraordinary miracles through Paul, so that even handkerchiefs and aprons that had touched him were taken to the sick, and their illnesses were cured and the evil spirits left them. – Acts 19:11-12

Praise God for His supernatural power that releases His possibilities in the middle of our impossibilities! Nothing is too difficult for God!

God's Glory Releases Creativity

14. The glory of God always sparks _____ within people.

15. In the beginning, God _____, and He is still continuing to create new things through you and me.

Reflection:

• What creative deposits has God's glory given you and what happened through them?

• If you haven't experienced this yet, then what areas of your life could benefit from this and how?

I believe that God wants you to be successful. The Holy Spirit wants to give you new creative ideas for success! He wants to give you new creative ideas for work and home – how to handle your finances; how to be a better husband or wife, son or daughter, mom or dad; how to worship Him; and how to become a soul-winner in the glory!

NOTES

 KEYS FOR ACTIVATION

Did you notice the connection between worship and manifestations of God's glory? It was while I was leading worship that I first had supernatural oil flow from my hands. On many occasions when gold dust appeared, it came after I worshiped God.

Praise and worship allows you to tap into the atmosphere of heaven. As you sing or speak worship from your spirit, you connect with God's Spirit, which allows Him to begin moving in your life. When we choose to worship God, He is enthroned over the location and circumstances where we are worshiping.

> *Yet you are holy, enthroned on the praises of Israel. – Psalm 22:3 (NLT)*

If you will give God thanks for the things He is doing in your life (instead of complaining about the things that are going wrong), you will begin to walk in new dimensions of supernatural power that will cause the manifestation of God's glory to come to you!

The Bible says that our thankfulness will open the door to rivers of blessing because we come into His gates with thanksgiving.

> *Enter his gates with thanksgiving and his courts with praise; give thanks to him and praise his name. – Psalm 100:4*

- Take time right now to think of the areas in your life where you would like God to manifest His glory. Be specific. What exactly do you need in those areas? What breakthrough needs to happen?

- Now start thanking the Lord for those things as though you have already received them. Thank Him until you feel His presence come, then praise Him for who He is. Praise Him for His goodness that brings the breakthrough you need!

You are enthroning Him over your circumstances, giving Him authority to do something about them, while at the same time releasing grace in your words that release the solutions you need by faith.

Your worship and declarations create a future for you filled with the things you need, and most of all, a future filled with God's glory!

APPLICATION AT HOME

In this lesson we've seen that the glory of God releases help in saving the lost, healings and deliverance, breakthrough in finances, miracles of creativity, wisdom in relationships, and so much more! Obviously we can all use more of God's glory in our lives! This increase in glory comes through worship – praise and thanksgiving.

- Write down the list you made in the Activation section and take time every day this week to speak or sing thanksgiving and praise to God over your circumstances.

- Look toward your future, thinking specifically about who you desire to become and what God has called you to. Remember prophetic words you've received and thank God for what He is speaking to you through them. Take hold of your glorious future by faith as you thank God for bringing you the things you need to get there and praising Him for being the God who will faithfully get you there.

- Keep notes each day of things you feel the Lord saying to you. Write down anything that happens in life to fulfill the things you have been thanking God for. These are testimonies of God's glory being manifested to you! Thank God for them no matter how small they are and greater glory will invade your life!

Lesson Three

SOUL WINNING IN THE GLORY

Objective: To equip each student with a powerful soul-winning strategy delivered by an angel.

Overview: Within this lesson, you will learn a divine technique for winning souls in the glory and hear faith-building testimonies of how this tool has been used to win the lost.

 ## HIDDEN REVELATION

When I was in my late teenage years, I read a mini-book by world-renowned healing evangelists Charles and Frances Hunter that changed my life forever! An angel actually came and sat down with the Hunters, sharing with them a brand new way that they could win the lost!

1. 2 Peter 3:9 says, "The Lord is not slow about His _____, as some understand slowness. He is _____ with you, not wanting anyone to _____, but everyone to come to _____."

Since reading that book, *There Are Two Kinds Of...,* I have taken this tool and used it all over the world.

2. This tool works _____ or _____ signs and wonders to accompany it.

I have ministered to many people with this technique and have found great success!

29

Notes

KEYS TO BECOMING A SUPERNATURAL SOUL WINNER [1]

3. Set a _____-_____ goal. God will meet your _____!

4. Ask the question: "There are _____ kinds of people: those who are _____ and those who are about to be. Which one are you?"

   If they say, "I'm saved" or "I'm the first one," then _____ with them.

   If they say, "I'm about to be," or "I'm the second one," _____ say, "_____ this after me."

5. Plant the seed of _____ in prayer. Have them repeat the following _____ after you:

   "Father, _____ my sins. Jesus, come into my _____. Make me the kind of _____ that You want me to be. Thank You for _____ me."

Points To Remember

6. Don't change the _____ the angel gave. Say, "Repeat after me!" If you say, "_____," you will _____ the sinner.

7. After they pray, always _____ them, "Where is _____ right now?" The answer should be: "In my _____!" If their answer is different then have them _____ the prayer after you again.

Reflection:

• What do you believe are the benefits of using this tool?

Notes

SOUL WINNING WITH A TELEMARKETER

When I first began using this "Two Kinds of" soul-winning technique, I received a phone call at home from a telemarketer. The Holy Spirit told me to listen to her entire message and then tell her that there are "two kinds of people." So I did as the Holy Spirit asked me to do.

8. God will set others up to receive something _____ from us!

9. The Spirit of God will begin _____ to you about creative ways to win _____ in the glory

By witnessing to that telemarketer, one more soul was added to the Kingdom of God!

Reflection:

- Think about times when the Holy Spirit prompted you to tell someone the gospel. How might those times have been different if you had used this tool?

SET A SOUL-WINNING GOAL

When you wake up in the morning, set a reasonable "soul-winning goal" for yourself and see how God will fulfill the desires of your heart.

10. Proverbs 29:18 says that people _____ without _____.

11. The opposite of that promises that when you have a _____, you will _____!

12. Many people within the church aren't winning _____ because they have not set a _____ for soul _____.

Give yourself a goal and watch the simple supernatural lifestyle come alive in your life!

NOTES

SOUL WINNING AT A HOTEL

As I was getting ready for a meeting one evening, gold dust began to appear all over me in the shower. When I left my hotel room and began walking down the hotel hallway, I noticed a friendly couple walking toward me. As the lady looked at me she said "You're really sparkling!" I said, "Yes! This is a miracle from God because Jesus loves you!" She looked at me again in bewilderment and asked, "But how did it get on you?"

13. God will give us opportunities to share His _____ and _____ with the world around us.

14. Every person is an _____!

15. God is giving us His _____ power to _____ the lost!

16. Romans 10:10 says, "For it is with your _____ that you believe and are _____, and it is with your _____ that you confess and are _____."

Right there in the hotel hallway I led this beautiful couple to know the saving power of salvation through Jesus Christ. This is simple supernatural!

KEYS FOR ACTIVATION

Write down a realistic soul-winning goal for this next week. Pray over your goal, thanking God for giving you everything you need to win souls for the Kingdom of God.

Get together with one to two other classmates and discuss how to encourage each other this next week as you step out toward meeting your goals. Pray for each other and share every testimony of what you see God do. Rejoicing with someone else in their victories sets you up for your own breakthrough, so thank God together for what He does!

APPLICATION AT HOME

Use the "Two Kind of People" tool, ask God to give you opportunities to lead people to salvation. Thank God every day for how He is going to help you accomplish your goals, then step out in faith whenever opportunities arise.

As you lead people to the Lord, rejoice and thank God. Immediately find other believers to rejoice with you in the testimony (contact your classmates and share your story with them). This will increase both their faith and yours while at the same time setting you up for even more salvation testimonies!

Lesson Four

RECEIVE THE POWER!

Objective: To release each student into the baptism of the Holy Spirit, marked by the power of God and the sign of speaking in tongues.

Overview: Within this lesson, you will learn why receiving the baptism in the Holy Spirit is necessary, receive instruction on the sign of speaking in tongues, and activate this gift by receiving the baptism in the Holy Spirit.

 HIDDEN REVELATION

One evening a Latin American woman approached me and told me that I had ministered salvation to her in her native Spanish dialect while I was singing in other tongues. As a sign for the unbeliever, the Lord allowed me to speak forth words of salvation, directed straight to that lady's heart. It was something completely arranged by the Holy Spirit!

1. The supernatural realm is not a _____ "add-on" in the life of a believer. It is _____!

She left the meeting that evening with a fresh promise of eternal peace, and I departed that church service with a renewed sense of awe for the realms of eternity.

2. As we abide in the _____ realm, the Lord will use us to _____ in ways that we would have never _____ possible.

THE SUPERNATURAL IS A MUST

A few years ago we recorded a live worship CD called "The Drink." Sometime later, when the CD was distributed, I received a letter from an Indian lady who listened to the CD and said she heard me singing in her native Hindi language. That woman was blessed by this Spirit-led message, and I was once again overwhelmed by the greatness of God's power.

NOTES

3. The Lord will give us various _____ languages as we begin _____ in the _____.

Reflection:

*   Why do you think the supernatural realm is a mandatory requirement in order to walk in the fullness of God's purposes for us here on the earth?

THE HOLY SPIRIT RELEASED TONGUES

In the second chapter of Acts, we read about the great power of the Holy Spirit that was released upon the early church, with the appearance of tongues of fire and the sound of a rushing wind.

> *All of them were filled with the Holy Spirit and began to speak in other tongues as the Spirit enabled them. – Acts 2:4*

One of the evidences of the baptism in the Holy Spirit is the manifestation of speaking in unknown tongues. It happened in the upper room and it's continuing to happen all over the world today!

4. When we receive the _____ in the Holy Spirit with the _____ of speaking in tongues, there are no _____ for what God may do with this new language.

5. The Holy Spirit is able to give you a tongue with _____ languages, _____ languages, _____ languages, or language only understood in the _____ of _____.

6. When we begin to pray with this new language, we call it "_____ in the _____" because the Spirit of God is _____ our prayers and intercession.

NOTES

Tongues Releases Heaven to Earth

One of the greatest revelations of the Spirit is that something is always happening in the glory realm. The activity of heaven is always moving!

7. Every time we speak in heavenly _____ something is moving from _____ to _____ into our spirit man.

8. These new tongues are even filled with _____ and _____!

9. Our _____ gifts are important, but they must be _____ to the flow of His Spirit so that they might become vibrantly _____ – awakened by the current move of the _____.

The baptism in the Holy Spirit releases us into the flow of heaven, opening up the glory realm.

Reflection:

- How is praying in tongues different from praying in a known language?

The Baptism in The Holy Spirit Releases Dynamite-Type Power

The Bible tells us that after the Holy Spirit filled those who were gathered in the upper room, they received a supernatural enablement with signs, wonders, and miracles following, and many people were added to the church on a daily basis.

> *But you will receive power when the Holy Spirit comes on you; and you will be my witnesses. – Acts 1:8*

10. The _____ in the Holy Spirit brings the _____ to work the _____ of God.

11. We are _____ up to the power source of _____ through the _____ in the Holy Spirit!

Notes

Without the baptism we will never be able to live up to our full potential in Christ. We must receive the baptism in the Holy Spirit in order to function as the witnesses that God has created us to be. This is simple supernatural.

The Father Gives the Holy Spirit to Those Who Ask

Luke 11:9-13 says that when we ask for the baptism in the Holy Spirit, we must rest assured in the promise of God. When we read this Scripture, we must believe that it is true.

12. Luke 11:9-10 says, "So I say to you…everyone who asks _____; he who seeks _____; and to him who _____, the door will be opened."

13. Luke 11:13 says, "If you then, though you are _____, know how to give _____ gifts to your children, how much more will your Father in _____ give the _____ _____to those who ask him!"

The Bible says that our Heavenly Father will give the Holy Spirit to those who ask for Him!

Reflection:

- According to Luke 11:9-13, what is the basis for us receiving the Holy Spirit – we being good children or God being a good Father?

- What does this say to you about God's nature as our Heavenly Father?

Open Your Mouth and He Will Fill It

I can't tell you how many people have asked to receive the baptism in the Holy Spirit, but then they keep their mouth closed when it's time for them to begin speaking in new tongues. When God desires to give us a new language we must open up our mouths in order for Him to fill it (Psalm 81:10).

NOTES

14. When we _____ to speak in tongues, it is often like when a _____ first learns to speak. We aren't usually experts right from the _____!

15. When we _____ for the baptism in the Holy Spirit and we _____ that we have received what we have prayed for, we can _____ up our mouth and trust that God will begin to _____ it with His _____ tongue.

Open up your mouth and God will fill it. At first it might sound like a bunch of goo-goos and ga-gas, but as you yield to the Spirit of God, suddenly you will break through into a free-flowing current of heavenly language that has no end!

KEYS TO RECEIVING AND MINISTERING THE BAPTISM IN THE HOLY SPIRIT:

16. You must _____ that it is available _____! (Luke 11:9-13)

17. Do not believe the _____ of the enemy that you're not _____ enough. The _____ of the Holy Spirit is what will help you live a _____ life pleasing unto the Lord. (Romans 8:13)

18. _____ to receive the baptism in the Holy Spirit with the _____ of speaking in _____ tongues.

19. _____ speaking in _____ as the Holy Spirit enables you! (Acts 2:4)

NOTES

 KEYS FOR ACTIVATION

PRAYER TO RECEIVE THE BAPTISM IN THE HOLY SPIRIT

Everyone pray this prayer out loud (to receive the baptism in the Holy Spirit for the first time or for a fresh baptism):

Father, in the name of Jesus, I thank You that by faith I have received the gift of salvation from You. I believe that Your Word is true and that You have promised me another gift as well – the gift of the Holy Spirit. You have said in Your Word that You would give the Holy Spirit to those that ask. So right now, by faith, I ask for this gift and I thank you for filling me with your wonderful Holy Spirit.

I receive by faith this supernatural empowerment from heaven. I believe that I am being baptized in the Holy Spirit just like those who were gathered in the upper room. I thank you for giving me a new language that I may speak in tongues to bring glory to Your name! I believe that I have received this supernatural baptism in the Holy Spirit! Amen!

Now your step of faith here is to open up your mouth and begin speaking syllables that you don't necessarily understand. This is just like a baby beginning to speak.

You can trust that the Holy Spirit within you will control what you say and make it into a beautiful heavenly prayer language. Sometimes you may only get one or two words at a time. Let the Holy Spirit develop this language for you – it will come word by word, from faith to faith!

Whether this is the first time to speak in tongues or the thousandth time, take time right now and open your mouth, letting God fill it with supernatural language from heaven!

Reflection:

- Record your experience speaking in tongues for the first time. What happened? Was it easy? Did it come right away? How did it make you feel? Now thank your Father for such a wonderful gift, no matter how dramatic your experience was – thankfulness is the gateway to more!

APPLICATION AT HOME

It's fairly common for doubts to try to creep in concerning our early experiences of speaking in tongues. This is a tactic of the enemy to stop us from using this powerful tool before we become confident in it. You will overcome any doubting or critical spirits that may try to hinder you from this experience by staying focused on the Word of God and making it a habit to pray in tongues each day.

Whether tongues is new or you have been speaking in tongues for years, for this next week, choose a consistent time of day, such as right away when you get up, while you shower, or on your way to work or school, and use that time to practice speaking in tongues. Record your experiences below. You will be encouraged as you see your gift grow and feel the presence of the Lord mark your days in increased measure!

Many helpful Scriptures for meditation are listed in *Simple Supernatural* on pages 84-90. Choose one or two of these that are particularly meaningful to you and intentionally bring them to mind throughout the day to fuel your faith as you pray in tongues.

Lesson Five

POWER TO HEAL THE SICK

Objective: To equip each student with the ability to demonstrate the healing power of God, following the example given to us by Jesus.

Overview: Within this lesson, you will see that as you pattern your life and ministry after Jesus' example, then you will begin to see the same miracles that Jesus worked.

 HIDDEN REVELATION

Now that you have received the baptism in the Holy Spirit, you have received the power of God to work miracles, signs, and wonders to bring glory to Jesus!

1. _____ the baptism in the Holy Spirit we will _____ for the sick, but _____ the baptism in the Holy Spirit we will _____ the sick!

2. Matthew 10:8 commands us to, "_____ the sick, _____ the lepers, _____ the dead, _____ out demons."

HEALING IS ALWAYS GOD'S WILL

God's Word is continually unfailing in effectiveness and operation. When we trust it and have faith in it, that revelation will produce a miracle.

3. It is _____ God's will to heal (Mark 1:40-41)!

4. It's _____ our responsibility to _____ questions that only _____ understands.

NOTES

5. It is simply our _____ to _____ the infallible Word of God.

Some people say, "Sister So-And-So was such a good Sunday school teacher. She faithfully played piano at church and she never missed a meeting. So why is she still sick?"

6. Our healing _____ depends upon what _____ have done.

7. It is a _____ work that was _____ by Jesus Christ at the _____ of Calvary.

Healing is something we can receive because of what He's done! If we believe it, we'll receive it!

SICKNESS IS NEVER THE WORK OF GOD

Sickness is never the work of God. Sickness is always the work of the devil.

8. We have the _____ and _____over every work of the devil (Luke 10:19)!

When evening came, many who were demon-possessed were brought to him, and he drove out the spirits with a word and healed all the sick. This was to fulfill what was spoken through the prophet Isaiah: "He took up our infirmities and carried our diseases."
– Matthew 8:16-17

Then Jesus went about all the cities and villages, teaching in their synagogues, preaching the gospel of the kingdom, and healing every sickness and every disease among the people.
– Matthew 9:35

Reflection:

• What does it mean to you that the Word of God says Jesus healed *all* who came to Him – *every* sickness or disease, no matter what?

NOTES

Jesus Is Our Example

Let's take a deeper look at Matthew 9:35. Because Jesus is our ultimate example, I want you to clearly see what He did and how He operated in this miraculous ministry. We can learn how to operate in this realm of glory as we pay attention to His methods and His ways.

Jesus Was Teaching

> *Then Jesus went about all the cities and villages, teaching in their synagogues.*
> *– Matthew 9:35*

Teaching is always systematic. The revelation is revealed line upon line, precept upon precept (Isaiah 28:10).

9. We can begin walking in _____ demonstration by _____ the Word.

10. We can do this by _____ the Word of God into every _____ of sickness, _____, or infirmity that we encounter.

There was a man in one of our recent classes who had been suffering with a constant buzzing in his ears for over twenty years. But as I read the Word of God in regard to healing, suddenly the buzzing instantly stopped and this man could hear once again with clarity.

11. The Word of God is a _____ Word!

12. As you _____ and _____ the Word of God, it releases _____ for that which is being spoken.

13. The Scriptures declare that _____ comes by the _____ of the Word!

There is not one person on earth who cannot receive the healing power of God into their situation. The necessary faith will come as we hear God's perspective on the situation by listening to His Word!

Notes

JESUS WAS PREACHING

…preaching the gospel of the kingdom… – Matthew 9:35

What is this message that comes from God's heavenly Kingdom?

14. In the Kingdom there is no _____ or _____! (Revelation 21:4)

15. In the Kingdom there is no _____, _____, or _____! (Revelation 7:17)

16. In the Kingdom there is no more _____! (Luke 20:36)

Preaching is not always systematic in nature as teaching is, but many times it is more prophetic in that it comes by inspiration. We become inspired to preach!

17. The _____ power of God's Holy Spirit was released as _____ began to teach and _____ to the people!

18. Faith for the _____ cannot come until you _____ the Word.

This is why it is important to teach and preach God's Word in order that faith would arise for the impossible!

19. Begin to speak to your _____ and _____ it to come in line with the _____ of God!

Do you know what happened as I prophesied to people's situations? We witnessed one person after another give testimony to the healing power of God!

JESUS WAS DEMONSTRATING

…and healing every sickness and every disease among the people. – Matthew 9:35

NOTES

Whenever we teach healing and we preach the healing power of God, we must make room for the demonstration of that power to be revealed.

> *And my speech and my preaching were not with persuasive words of human wisdom, but in demonstration of the Spirit and of power. – 1 Corinthians 2:4*

At the Intensified Glory Institute we always make an opportunity for each student to receive their healing miracles by demonstrating what has been taught and preached.

20. After _____ and _____ the healing _____ of God, we must make room to _____ this power!

Jesus shows us how to help people step into their miracle:

21. He told the _____ man to go wash his _____. (John 9:7)

22. He told the _____ man to stand up and _____! (Matthew 9:6-7)

23. He told the _____ to go according to His _____. (Luke 17:14)

These simple acts of faith become a point of contact for the miracles to be demonstrated!

> *And it happened that the father of Publius lay sick of a fever and dysentery. Paul went in to him and prayed, and he laid his hands on him and healed him. So when this was done, the rest of those on the island who had diseases also came and were healed. – Acts 28:8-9*

At times people do not see the miracles because they haven't looked for them. Open your eyes and begin to look for the miracle.

24. Do not look for the _____.

25. Do not look for the _____.

26. Do not look for the _____.

27. Look for the _____ and you will _____ them! (Luke 11:9-10)

When you preach the Word, it becomes alive and begins to manifest!

NOTES

KEYS TO MINISTERING GOD'S HEALING POWER TO THE SICK:

28. You must _____ that healing is _____ today! (Hebrews 13:8)

29. Begin to _____ the Word of God in regard to healing by speaking _____ Scriptures. This will impart faith (Romans 10:17).

30. Begin to _____ the Word of God in regard to _____. Speak _____ to the body and _____ it to line up with the Word of God (Matthew 17:20).

31. _____ on the Word and begin to _____ something you could not do before! This will release the _____ manifestation (James 1:22).

 KEYS FOR ACTIVATION

1. Choose a partner and then choose one of the verses on healing from the book *Simple Supernatural*, pages 109-122.
2. Take turns teaching the verse you have chosen (you may both choose a different verse). This doesn't have to be an in depth teaching; you're simply declaring the truth of the Word.

An easy way to do this is to read the verse once, then go back through it more slowly, saying out loud anything the Lord highlights to your attention. Focus on these supernaturally highlighted sections and expand on them, saying whatever comes to mind about them. Just open your mouth and let God fill it!

As you speak out the truth of God's Word, His Spirit will come upon you and inspire you. Soon you will begin to preach! Again, just speak out whatever comes to you. The purpose of this exercise is not to produce a well-formed teaching or sermon, it is to help you recognize the flow of the Holy Spirit as He moves through you to bring revelation, faith, and healing to another person.

3. Remember to make room for the power of God to be demonstrated in your partner's life. If there is any area that needs healing – inside or outside their body – be sure to pray for and command healing to come into their circumstance.

4. After one person has done this, switch and let the other partner take their turn.

 APPLICATION AT HOME

Teaching and preaching are like muscles – the more you use them, the stronger they will get and the easier they will be to use. Just like speaking in tongues, as you practice, your abilities will grow.

Each day this week, choose a different verse on healing from *Simply Supernatural*, pages 109-122. Teach it and preach it just as you did with your partner – with a trusted friend or to yourself in the mirror. If possible, find someone who needs healing so that you may also practice the demonstration of power.

You'll find that the inspiration to preach will come more easily the more you practice. This will also cause these verses on healing to be written inside of you so that as you go through life – shopping, working, traveling, etc. – you will be able to use them to bring healing to those around you who need it.

Lesson Six

SEVEN KEYS TO THE GLORY REALM

Objective: To teach the seven keys that give us access to the glory realm.

Overview: Within this lesson, you will learn seven keys to the glory realm along with Scriptures that support each key.

 ## HIDDEN REVELATION

1. FAITH IN JESUS CHRIST

While there are many ways to enter into the spirit realm, there is only one way into the realm of the glory – through faith in Jesus Christ. In order to access the glory realm, you MUST have faith in Jesus Christ!

1. The way to hell is _____ and its gate is _____, but the only way to enter God's Kingdom is very _____ and _____ (Matthew 7:13-14).

2. Jesus is the _____, the _____, the _____, and the only way to the _____ (John 14:6).

3. We are made _____ of God when we put our _____ in Christ Jesus, and have now received His _____, making us no longer _____, but _____ of God Himself (Galatians 3:26, 4:6-7)!

4. As soon as we _____ in Jesus Christ, we are made _____ with God, no matter _____ we are (Romans 3:22).

Notes

Jesus is the ultimate manifestation of God's glory:

5. Jesus is God in _____ form, and He showed us the perfect picture of the Father's _____ through His unfailing _____ and _____ (John 1:14).

Reflection:

- If Jesus is the complete manifestation of God's glory, then what part does He play in our pursuit of the glory realm?

2. Believe The Word Of God

We need to have a relationship with God that goes beyond our natural sense realm and moves us into the "supernatural" sense realm of believing God's Word by faith. In order to walk in the glory realm, you must believe the Word of God!

6. Jesus said that those who _____ without seeing are _____. The Word of God is written so that we might _____ in Jesus and have _____ by the power of His _____ (John 20:27-31).

Believing the Word will cause you to live in the realm of glory:

7. When we _____ the Lord and do _____ then we will _____ (Psalm 37:3).

The "signs" or evidence of the glory realm will begin to manifest and follow you as you simply believe:

8. Jesus promised that those who believe will cast out _____, speak new _____, handle _____ with safety, drink poison without _____, and _____ the sick as confirmation of the words they _____ (Mark 16:15-20).

Notes

Reflection:

- How have you seen the Word of God lead you into His glory in your life?

3. Unity, Honor, and Blessing

God desires for us to dwell together in **unity**:

9. Jesus prayed that we would be _____ in the same way that He and the _____ are one. To accomplish this, He has given us His _____, and the result of our perfect _____ will be that the _____ will know that _____ came and that He _____ them (John 17:20-26).

10. Psalm 133:1-3 says, "How wonderful and pleasant it is when _____ live together in _____! For harmony is as precious as the anointing _____ that was poured over Aaron's head, that ran down his _____ and onto the border of his _____. Harmony is as _____ as the dew from Mount Hermon that falls on the mountains of _____. And there the Lord has pronounced his _____, even life _____."

11. It is _____ for followers of Christ Jesus to live in _____ harmony, so that with _____ voice we can give _____ and _____ to God (Romans 15:5-6).

God wants us to **honor** those around us – our fathers and mothers, and those who have gone before us in the faith:

12. The key to long _____ filled with _____ is to _____ our fathers and mothers (Deuteronomy 5:16).

NOTES

Bless those around you:

13. God _____ us so that we will be a _____ to others (Genesis 12:2).

Reflection:

- Is it possible to enter the fullness of God's glory by ourselves? Why or why not?

4. Holiness, Righteousness, and Humility

As we ask the Lord to visit us with His anointing of holiness, righteousness, and humility, we will receive an impartation that will cause us to access the glory realm at a greater degree than ever before:

14. 1 Peter 2:9 says, "But you are not like that, for you are a _____ people. You are _____ priests, a _____ nation, God's very own _____. As a result, you can show others the _____ of God, for he called you out of the _____ into his wonderful _____."

We must come before the Lord with humility:

15. We must be like Jesus, who did not _____ to being equal to God, but instead _____ himself as a slave, even to the point of dying on a _____. God so delighted in this attitude that He _____ Jesus to the place of _____ honor so that one day every creature will call Him _____ (Philippians 2:5-11).

16. Proverbs 22:4 says, "True _____ and _____ of the Lord lead to riches, _____, and long _____."

NOTES

17. Luke 14:11 says, "For those who _____ themselves will be _____, and those who _____ themselves will be _____."

Reflection:

• Holiness, righteousness, and humility express the character of God. In what way do they bring us into the glory realm?

5. Do Not Be Moved by Persecutions

When we are persecuted for His name's sake, we are blessed and will receive heavenly treasures and rewards!

18. When we are _____ for doing right, God gives us the _____ of Heaven; He _____ us when people mistreat us for being His _____. For this reason we should be _____ and very _____ (Matthew 5:10-12)!

19. We should be _____ and _____ for joy when people persecute us because great _____ awaits us in _____ (Luke 6:22-23)

20. Romans 12:14 says, "_____ those who persecute you. Don't _____ them; _____ that God will bless them."

Reflection:

• Why does choosing to bless and not curse, to be thankful and not grumble, lead us into the glory realm?

NOTES

6. Praise and Worship

Your praise changes the atmosphere and your worship sustains that realm! Praise and worship are the keys that unlock the pathway into the glory realm.

21. God's will for us is to _____ be joyful and _____ in _____ circumstances (1 Thessalonians 5:16, 18).

22. When the Lord shows His _____ to the nations then everyone will _____ Him (Isaiah 61:11)!

23. Acts 16:25-26 says, "Around midnight Paul and Silas were _____ and _____ hymns to God, and the other prisoners were listening. Suddenly, there was a massive _____, and the prison was _____ to its foundations. All the doors immediately flew _____, and the _____ of every prisoner fell off!"

Reflection:

• Describe an experience you had in praise and worship where you felt like you encountered God's glory or had a major breakthrough in your life.

7. Generosity

Your generosity opens up a realm of blessing, favor, and increase that causes the abundance of heaven's bounty to fill your life! If we want to imitate the example of Christ, we must learn how to be generous.

24. Deuteronomy 16:17 says, "All must _____ as they are able, according to the _____ given to them by the Lord your God."

Notes

25. Proverbs 3:9 says, "Honor the Lord with your _____ and with the _____ part of _____ you produce."

26. If we only _____ a little then we will reap a _____, but if we plant _____ then we will get a generous _____ (2 Corinthians 9:6).

27. Luke 6:38 says, "Give, and you will _____. Your gift will _____ to you in full – pressed _____, shaken together to make room for _____, running over, and _____into your lap. The amount you _____ will determine the amount you _____ back."

28. Jesus told us that it is more _____ to give than to _____ (Acts 20:35).

Reflection:

- God doesn't ask anything of us that He doesn't demonstrate Himself, and John 3:16 tells us that God so loved the world that He gave! What is it about generosity that makes it a key to the glory realm?

 KEYS FOR ACTIVATION

Let's take time to be activated into each of the keys of the glory realm.

1. **Faith in Jesus Christ.** Faith in Jesus is not just a onetime act; it is a recurring choice. The Word of God teaches that our faith can grow and that each of us has been given a measure of faith. What is God calling you to in life right now that you need faith to accomplish? Choose right now to believe in God for all you need and ask Him to increase your faith as you step into what He has for you.

2. **Believe the Word of God.** What does God's Word say about you? What does God's Word say about what God has called you to? What prophetic words have you received? Look to the other side of these words as though they were already complete and fulfilled in your life. What do you look like? What are you doing?

Now realize that what you are picturing is what God had in mind when He said those words. The vision you have in your mind has already been in God's, and it's why He spoke those words to you. Write down the vision of yourself that you see.

3. **Unity, Honor, and Blessing.** Jesus only has one body, and it isn't supposed to be divided through broken relationships. Can you think of anyone in the body of Christ with whom you have a broken or unhealthy relationship? Take time now and offer yourself to God for the sake of bringing reconciliation in that relationship.

Can you think of anyone who has gone before you into the areas to which you are called? Write their names down and ask God to give you creative ways to honor them.

Also, ask God for creative ways to honor your own parents. This is a huge key to His glory!

4. **Holiness, Righteousness, and Humility.** Holiness, righteousness, and humility come as we receive revelations of God, because as we see Him then we are transformed into the same image (2 Corinthians 3:18). Think of one or two areas of your life where you want to look more like Jesus. Now ask God to give you revelations of Himself in those areas (i.e. if you struggle with lying, then ask for a revelation of God as the Word of Truth).

5. **Do Not Be Moved by Persecutions.** Is there anyone who has ever persecuted you in any way for your faith in Jesus or your expression of love to Him (this happens outside and inside the church)? Choose to forgive them and declare blessings over them, releasing heaven to invade their lives!

6. **Praise and Worship.** Look over your answers to the previous 5 activations. In what areas do you want God to manifest His glory? Choose two or three of those areas to focus on and begin to praise God over those issues. Praise Him for His attributes that will bring the necessary change and thank Him that the change is coming!

7. **Generosity.** It's been said that the best way to overcome selfishness is to give. Are there any areas of your life where you see yourself acting primarily in your interest instead of in the interest of others? Talk to God about this and ask Him what He would have you give in those areas. Then give joyfully as He leads you to give (with money, time, talents, words, etc.).

APPLICATION AT HOME

Write below one or two of the activation steps that you felt the Lord highlight to you most during class.

Look for ways to take action on them this week. For example, if there is a broken relationship keeping you from unity in the body of Christ and God opens the door to reconcile with that person, then don't just keep praying for unity, go do something to make it happen! Or if you are praying about how to give generously toward a specific area of your life, believe that an opportunity to give will come up, and when it does then give generously!

Remember that we are supposed to live from the dimension of the glory realm. In the glory realm we will produce greater results. Put these seven keys into practice and flow in the glory realm. In the glory, God will produce a greater harvest through us as we yield to His Word and His ways. Expect that as you are faithful to use them that God's Glory will invade your life and circumstances!

Lesson Seven

THE COMMISSION

Objective: To commission you into supernatural soul winning and healing the sick through the power of Jesus with the baptism in the Holy Spirit.

Overview: In this lesson you will see that Jesus' commissioning of His disciples is your commissioning too.

 HIDDEN REVELATION

Mark 16:17-18 have been key verses throughout this class:

1. "And these _____ will accompany those who believe: In my name they will _____ out demons; they will _____ in new tongues; they will pick up _____ with their hands; and when they drink _____ poison, it will not hurt them at all; they will place their hands on _____ people, and they will get _____."

It's important for us to understand these verses in the context they are given, because they follow a very important command from Jesus.

2. Jesus said, "_____ into all the world and _____ the good news to all _____. Whoever believes and is _____ will be _____, but whoever does not _____ will be condemned."
    – Mark 16:16

Now listen to what happened after Jesus gave this command to His first disciples:

3. "Then the _____ went out and preached _____, and the Lord _____ with them and confirmed his word by the _____ that accompanied it." – Mark 16:20

77

NOTES

The signs we have talked about throughout this class came as the disciples obeyed Jesus' command to go. If you have accepted Jesus Christ as your Lord and Savior, then you are a disciple of Christ and He is commissioning you too!

4. Jesus didn't say to _____ put, fasten your _____, or to be _____ in the church pew.

5. Jesus said to "_____!"

NOTES

 KEYS FOR ACTIVATION

This is the commission that He is giving you today. Jesus even said that you would do greater miracles than He did on the earth! Write below what "greater miracles" could look like in your own life.

6. "Verily, verily, I say unto you, He that _____ on me, the _____ that I do shall he do also; and _____ works than these shall he do; because I go unto my Father." – John 14:12 (KJV)

As you have taken this class, I pray that you have felt the anointing of God filling you with His strength. Believe it! Receive it! Now, I give you my blessing to... Go and do it!!!

This is simple supernatural!

7. "But don't just _____ to God's word. You must _____ what it says. Otherwise, you are only _____ yourselves." – James 1:22 (NLT)

APPLICATION AT HOME

The tools you have received in this class have world-changing power! As you have done the application at home each week, you have seen God's glory manifest and the supernatural happening through your hands and words.

My desire is that you would continue to practice all of these things. Take time this week to review the ways you applied what you learned in class. Seek the Lord about how He wants you to incorporate what you have learned into your daily life. Remember that they are not just tools for class, but also tools for life! Turn these learning experiences and world-changing tools into habits and become a world-changer!

STUDY GUIDE ANSWERS

LESSON ONE:
YOU ARE SUPERNATURAL!

1. on purpose
2. same, forever
3. believe, do
4. do, results
5. recover
6. free
7. languages, tongues
8. light, heart
9. redeemed, purified, eager
10. demons, tongues, snakes, poison, heal
11. being, purpose, ways of heaven
12. we are trespassing
13. we are invading the earth
14. results

LESSON TWO:
SIGNS & WONDERS

1. preach, Gospel, harvest, souls
2. talents, abilities
3. glory
4. temple, in
5. thoughts, ways
6. through, signs
7. glory
8. increasing
9. love
10. saying, faith, love
11. fragrance
12. aroma
13. anoints, oil, overflow
14. creativity
15. created

LESSON THREE:
SOUL WINNING IN THE GLORY

1. promise, patient, perish, repentance
2. with, without
3. soul-winning, faith
4. two, saved, rejoice, immediately, Repeat
5. salvation, prayer, forgive, heart, person, saving
6. wording, Pray, scare
7. ask, Jesus, heart, repeat
8. great
9. speaking, souls
10. perish, vision
11. vision, prosper
12. souls, goal, winning
13. love, glory
14. opportunity
15. supernatural, win
16. heart, justified, mouth, saved

LESSON FOUR:
RECEIVE THE POWER!

1. luxury, mandatory
2. glory, minister, dreamed
3. unknown, singing, Spirit
4. baptism, evidence, limitations
5. foreign, ancient, future, realms, heaven
6. praying, Spirit, directing
7. tongues, heaven, earth
8. health, healing
9. natural, surrendered, alive, Spirit
10. baptism, enablement, works
11. hooked, heaven, baptism
12. receives, finds, knocks
13. evil, good, heaven, Holy Spirit

14. begin, baby, start
15. pray, believe, open, fill, supernatural
16. believe, today
17. lie, good, infilling, holy
18. Pray, evidence, new
19. Begin, faith

LESSON FIVE:
POWER TO HEAL THE SICK

1. Without, pray, with, heal
2. Heal, cleanse, raise, cast
3. always
4. not, answer, God
5. responsibility, believe
6. never, we
7. completed, finished, cross
8. power, authority
9. supernatural, teaching
10. speaking, situation, illness
11. healing
12. teach, preach, faith
13. faith, hearing
14. sickness, disease
15. pain, sorrow, suffering
16. death
17. healing, Jesus, preach
18. miraculous, hear
19. body, command, Word
20. teaching, preaching, power, demonstrate
21. blind, eyes
22. crippled, walk
23. lepers, word
24. sickness
25. disease
26. pain
27. miracles, find

28. believe, available
29. teach, healing
30. preach, healing, prophetically, command
31. Act, do, visible

LESSON SIX:
SEVEN KEYS TO THE GLORY REALM

1. broad, wide, narrow, difficult
2. Way, Truth, Life, Father
3. children, faith, Spirit, slaves, heirs
4. believe, right, who
5. human, glory, love, faithfulness
6. believe, blessed, believe, life, name
7. trust, good, prosper
8. demons, languages, snakes, harm, heal, received
9. one, Father, Spirit, unity, world, Jesus, loved
10. brothers, harmony, oil, beard, robe, refreshing, Zion, blessing, everlasting
11. fitting, complete, one, praise, glory
12. life, blessing, honor
13. blessed, blessing
14. chosen, royal, holy, possession, goodness, darkness, light
15. cling, humbled, cross, elevated, highest, Lord
16. humility, fear, honor, life
17. exalt, humbled, humble, exalted
18. persecuted, treasures, blessed, followers, happy, glad
19. happy, leap, reward, heaven
20. Bless, curse, pray
21. always, rejoice, all
22. justice, praise
23. praying, singing, earthquake, shaken, open, chains

24. give, blessings
25. wealth, best, everything
26. sow, little, generously, harvest
27. receive, returned, down, more, poured, give, get
28. blessed, receive
- Reflection Question Answer: Generosity is a key to the glory realm because God is generous. When we are like the Glorious One then we will access His glory.

LESSON SEVEN: THE COMMISSION

1. signs, cast, speak, snakes, deadly, sick, well
2. Go, preach, creation, baptized, saved, believe
3. disciples, everywhere, worked, signs
4. stay, seatbelt, comfortable
5. Go
6. believeth, works, greater
7. listen, do, fooling

For more information about live training seminars,
The Intensified Glory Institute®, and other glory resources,
please contact the ministry of Joshua & Janet Angela Mills

Toll-free 1-866-60-NEW-WINE
Online 24/7 www.NewWineInternational.org